WHAT WERE THEIR DREAMS?

Valleys of Hope and Pain: Canada's History

What Were Their Dreams?

Valleys of Hope and Pain: Canada's History

Wendy Morton

Black Moss Press
2009

Library and Archives Canada Cataloguing in Publication
Morton, Wendy, 1940-
    What were their dreams : valleys of hope and pain : Canada's history / Wendy Morton.
Poems.
ISBN 978-0-88753-460-7
    1. Indians of North America--British Columbia--Poetry. I. Title.
PS8576.O778W59 2009   C811'.6   C2009-902306-7

Published by Black Moss Press at 2450 Byng Road, Windsor, Ontario, N8W 3E8. Canada. Black Moss books are distributed in Canada and the U.S. by LitDistCo. All orders should be directed there.

Black Moss would like to acknowledge the generous financial assistance to its publishing program from both the Canada Council for the Arts and the Ontario Arts Council.

Second Printing, January 2010

ONTARIO ARTS COUNCIL
CONSEIL DES ARTS DE L'ONTARIO

Le Conseil des Arts | The Canada Council
du Canada | for the Arts

PRINTED IN CANADA

CONTENTS

Over

The story of Port Alberni provides a snapshot of the larger stories of British Columbia and of Canada. They all reflect an attempt to construct a social and physical environment in which a certain dream could be realized. Broadly, it was an immigrant dream, in which people were "pulled" to a place by economic opportunities. For those willing to accept the challenge of moving and refashioning their lives, this offered the prospect of social mobility – better lives for them and their children. To foster such a dream, certain conditions had to be created, based on the values of liberty, equality, and property that shaped Canadian political and legal systems. Although encouraging the dream of immigrants to make Canada home, at times the process of country-building has presented barriers to the full participation of certain groups, such as First Nations and Asian or Black immigrants. Today, efforts are being made to ensure that such barriers are removed, so that all our dreams are encouraged, and we can share equally in building our future.

Like British Columbia, the city of Port Alberni has been shaped by 150 years of development that started with the 1858 Fraser River gold rush. Since then, three major periods of growth and prosperity, one roughly every fifty years, have inspired the dreams of residents and newcomers. Their dreams are reflected in today's city.

In 1858 the Fraser River gold rush focused attention on BC and Vancouver Island. Few achieved wealth, but the dream of riches meant BC became identified as a "land of opportunity" for immigrants. Some entrepreneurs turned to other resources provided by the region's forests, mines, and fisheries. In 1859 the Victoria-based commission merchant Edward Stamp chose Alberni, with its timber resources and Pacific access, for his dream of building the first major export sawmill in the region. After shipping over 11 million feet of lumber to South America, China, and Hawaii, the then-owners, Anderson & Company, unable to retain workers, abandoned the operation in 1865, but kept the land.

In 1858 the Alberni Valley was home to two Nuu-chah-nulth nations, the Hupacasath and the Tseshaht, who, other than sharing in the salmon runs of the Somass River, lived in and utilized the region in different ways. For both nations, there existed an essential link between place or land, resources, and people, and although they developed distinct societies, both nations considered the Alberni Valley their homeland. Their dream of home began to change with Stamp's competing dream of a sawmill. Supported by the guns of the supply ships and a payment of £20 worth of goods, Stamp convinced the Tseshaht to move their settlement at the mill site to a location further up the river, today the main Tseshaht reserve.

By the early 1880s, the federal government laid out reserves for the Hupacasath and Tseshaht Nations. This not only limited access to the lands and resources these nations required to maintain their traditional economies, but defined which lands were available for newcomers to claim. Additionally, the amended Indian Act of 1884 included provisions intended to assimilate First Nations, replacing indigenous culture, as well as taking away lands and resources. First, certain key ceremonies, such as the potlatch, were banned as being contrary to the values of the dominant society. Second, the federal government funded various Christian denominations to operate a system of day schools and residential schools, with the goal of assimilating First Nations children. The residential schools were total institutions, in which the children were to learn to speak English, become Christian, receive a basic education emphasizing "practical" skills, and renounce their own cultural traditions. Characterized as ineffective, harsh, and unsafe, the residential schools created an environment that made psychological, sexual, and physical abuse common. Although the Alberni Indian Residential School closed in 1973, a legacy of pain remains evident among its survivors.

The state was transforming the region from an Aboriginal homeland to a place to attract the land-seeking immigrants from eastern Canada expected with the completion of the Canadian Pacific Railway [CPR] in 1886. In anticipation, the English firm of Anderson & Company, which retained most of its 2,000 acre sawmill land grant, laid out an Alberni townsite in 1886. In 1905, it formed the Alberni Land Company to manage sales, and within two years struck a deal with the CPR-owned Esquimalt & Nanaimo Railway [E&N] to extend a rail line to the new sawmills on the harbour at "New Alberni," already served by the CPR-owned Canadian Pacific Navigation Company. In 1909 the Alberni Land Company began further townsite development, expecting to profit from industrial growth and improved access.

In 1908 Alberni enjoyed the economic benefits of the "Second Industrial Revolution," when consumer demand, new technology, and mass production meant growing markets for raw materials including base metals, forest products, and food products. The Prairie wheat boom drove Canada's economy, and BC lumber built Prairie cities and farms. This brought a new wave of

Canadian and British immigrants, often attracted by the promotions of local "boosters." Alberni had its share of these boosters, selling the region with dreams of prosperity. They emphasized the surrounding forest, mineral, and marine resources, and Alberni's geographical location as a "gateway to the Pacific," now with rail and road connections as well.

Two settlements competed for regional dominance, with Old Alberni, as the service centre for agricultural settlement in the region, falling behind "New" or Port Alberni, with its industry and transportation links. The latter became the official terminus of the E&N in 1911. As the rivalry continued, the population of the Albernis rose to over 4,000, and both the cities incorporated in 1912-1913. Some infrastructure, like telephone and electrical services, and many new commercial and residential buildings, appeared in this period.

Although affected by the Great Depression, the Albernis soon recovered, due to the strength of the forest industry. In 1935 Bloedel, Stewart & Welch built the Somass Mill, and the following year the H.R. MacMillan Export Company bought the Alberni Pacific Lumber Company. The industry expanded during WWII. H.R. MacMillan Export, by now the dominant regional forest company, built the Alberni Plywood Division in 1942, followed by opening the Alberni Pulp & Paper Mill in 1947. H.R. MacMillan Export continued to expand its holdings, in 1951 merging with

Bloedel, Stewart & Welch as MacMillan & Bloedel, Ltd. The Albernis depended on the forest industry, and the regional forest industry <u>was</u> MacMillan & Bloedel.

In 1958 Alberni and Port Alberni flourished. Pent-up demand following the Depression and WWII, and the postwar "baby boom," meant that consumer spending took off, led by suburban development and the automobile industry. The forest industry expanded to provide the materials to build the suburbs. Dreaming of prosperity, a new wave of immigrants, from Canada or war-torn Europe, was attracted to the Albernis. In the 1960s Port Alberni vied with the auto-building cities of Ontario for the highest per-capita income in Canada.

In the Albernis transportation changed, as the last passenger train ran in 1957, and logging trucks replaced trains in the forest industry. Road development resulted in the opening of the West Coast Highway in 1959, connecting Alberni to the transcontinental system. Services and amenities improved, leaving us with facilities like Echo Centre and the Port Alberni City Hall. Many chose to raise families in Port Alberni during the baby boom, and their needs were met by new hospitals and schools. A strong economy made the dream of home ownership possible, and new residential districts developed, with features like the wide streets distinct to the city. Acknowledging the economic power of the community, the Woodward's chain opened a department store in 1948, followed by many other retailers. Finally, in 1967 Alberni and

Port Alberni amalgamated into today's City of Port Alberni.

In 2009 Port Alberni is in transition. Due to global trends beginning in the 1970s and continuing to the present day, traditional resource industries are in decline. The people of Port Alberni are taking the first steps to move into a post-industrial economy. The rich environment that supported export industry, and the distinct history and culture that evolved, now provide attractions for tourism.

As the importance of industry fades, the city of Port Alberni changes. The commercial centre of the city is shifting from the "uptown" district to the Johnson Street or Highway 4 corridor. The emphasis is now on strip development featuring big-box and chain stores, while trying to find solutions to revitalize older business districts. Concessions made to retain industry raise concerns over residential tax burdens. Meanwhile, there is a certain reluctance to fully engage in a post-industrial economy – the golden years of the forest industry remain a strong memory in the community. However, there is a bright note. Now with some of the lowest real estate prices on Vancouver Island, Port Alberni is bringing homebuyers from other regions, resulting in some new subdivisions and more construction. Once again, people are attracted to Port Alberni in pursuit of their dreams, and will leave their imprint on the city.

Jamie Morton
BC Historian

Pre

This book has grown from the exhibition, "What Were Their Dreams: Port Alberni 1858 – 2008", developed and produced by Alberni Valley Museum staff and presented at the Museum March 27 through September 28, 2008. The exhibit provided an opportunity for our museum staff to try several new approaches, including the exciting prospect of working with a poet and conveying ideas about history via the medium of poetry.

Wendy Morton's connection with Port Alberni began with her involvement with Forest Fest, a summer celebration of spoken word held annually at our McLean Mill National Historic Site.

Delighted by the poem Wendy created from the find of a 1922 B.C. Directory, and read at the opening Forest Fest in 2007, I invited her to be part of the team I was forming to create an exhibit on local history. At that point the exhibit was called 'On the Street Where You Live' and explored town growth through a recent donation of photographs from the City Works department.

The curatorial team who wove together the many threads of this exhibit were: Dr. Jamie Morton, BC Historian; Ken Rutherford, Heritage Commission Chair and long time Port Albernian; Guy Cicon, City of Port Alberni Engineer; Scott Smith City of Port Alberni planner; Wendy Morton and Alberni Valley Museum Curators Cindy Van Volsem, Shelley Harding and Kirsten Smith, along with myself.

Wendy Morton wrote twenty poems inspired by research into our community's written history and the Museum's photographic archives. She was provided with journals and images from our collection. Poems appeared throughout the exhibit, in large letters on the walls, superimposed on photographs, printed on index type cards you might find in an engineering office or inside copies of early promotional brochures and tucked into pockets secured to walls.

Our exhibit gave voice to many who had not been heard publicly before. Those such as anonymous faces in photographs from the Museum collection; generic contributions to stories of early life; First Nations; and city workers – the men, then, who actually filled the holes, built the bridges and created the streets for the new subdivisions as our community grew to a city.

The poems gave us all a way to imagine the lives of those individuals and they gave all our visitors a new way to access history. Placing local history in the broader context of 150 years of BC history provided an understanding of the waves of immigration and the forces that brought people to this area and the economic circumstances that impacted the way in which our community grew.

Over the run of the exhibit Wendy visited the community, offering to write poems in exchange for personal stories.

The project then expanded from an invitation to imagine experiences of the past, to the opportunity to hear new forms of stories from people we know and to consider an even broader view of our community's cultural history.

We thank the organizations who provide financial support to the Museum: the City of Port Alberni and the Province of BC through the BC Arts Council; and the funders of the 'Dreams' exhibit: BC 150 Local Museums Program and the BC Museums Association.

Jean McIntosh, MA
Director, Alberni Valley Museum
Port Alberni, British Columbia

Fore

word

As a curator of the Alberni Valley Museum collection, I care for photographs relevant to the history of the Alberni Valley on Vancouver Island. There are photographs that document the history of our valley from the mundane to the exceptional. People come to our museum looking for these photographs. Sometimes they find an image of a relative, a home, a friend. I have seen tears of joy in a woman when finding the only photo of her grandmother that she had ever seen. I have also seen a man cry when facing an image of his abuser in a Residential School photograph.

Images and words comprise this assemblage of history and the lives of people who passed through this valley, living their dreams. We keep these images for people to remember and, in some cases, to come to terms with the past. Is it worthwhile to spend time and money caring for fragile images? It is, because they are meaningful and because they evoke memory. Sometimes, a happy reunion of mind and image: a renewed memory. And sometimes, a painful memory, still.

This project joined images and words to create glimpses of our shared history: the dreams of the past, present and future. I was initially resistant to using poetry to convey history in this exhibit. But, as the poems were written by Wendy Morton and forwarded to me, I saw immediate connections to images I knew we had in the collection. For example, the poem *Say These Words* could have been illustrated by any of the concepts in it, such as First Nations traditional life or territorial scenery. We could have used photos of the children dressed as angels in a Christmas play, of parents saying goodbye as the children head off to school, of students holding musical instruments. But it was the little girls walking behind their teacher under the mountain known now as Arrowsmith that truly illustrated the words for me. With the poems in front of me, I had the joy of finding the photographs that embraced the words, and in a sense created photo-poems that draw those who see them into the history of this valley. And in a real sense, the history of Canada.

Cindy van Volsem
Curator, Alberni Valley Museum
Port Alberni, British Columbia

The Exhibit

WHAT WERE THEIR DREAMS?

The settlers: the Scots, the English, the Irish,
the Eastern Canadians, the Chinese, the old soldiers
of the Boer war,
the remittance men.
They held in their hands a double-bitted axe,
a broad axe,
a cross-cut saw,
a straw cutter.
They came to the cedar flats,
the alder flats, the swamp land of wild grass and rushes.
Drained it. Built split cedar culverts.
Cleared the forests, stumped and burned.
For the house.
For the farm.
For the dream.

THE HOMES

Cedar. Fir. Shake roofs.
Built high. The creek nearby.
Or the well. They carried buckets
to the house. Stocked the root cellar:
potatoes, carrots, turnips, beets.
Kept pigs, chickens.
Their fences, stumps.
They kept oxen, horses.
A cow. The slow days.
The rain. The fire of their dreams.

Creamery Road Alberni Vancouver Island

THE FARM

Hay cut by scythe and cradle,
turned and dried,
raked into windrows, cured in the sun,
hand pitched into wagons,
forked into the barn.
Oxen and stone boat for rock
moving, then stump pulling
with a mallet lever.
Shingles made with frow and maul,
planks split with glut and bettle.
Two men on the pit saw.
Harvest: root cellar filled;
pigs butchered, the meat salted, smoked.
Lard boiled up.
Eggs in waterglass.
Apples dried.
Butter salted before
the cows went dry.

TAKE THESE NAMES FOR DREAMS

Green Mountain, Red Rose, Carmen, Late Rose,
Gold Coin, Myatt.
Potatoes: 1 buck a hundred pounds.
Purple Tops, Valentian: turnips.
A buck twenty-five a hundred pounds.
Hand-pulped Mangold
for the cattle, the poultry.
Red Fife, Marquis, the wheat.
First you dream.

J. BURKE, ALBERNI LIVERY

Across from the Arlington Hotel,
a red sign, " Livery Barn, J. Burke, Prop."
A hay loft, 3 teams of horses,
one race horse, riding horses.
A wagon, sulkies, buggies, a democrat,
a buckboard.
A buck a day to board your horse.
Out front, an easy chair,
a plank bench.
The old timers talked land clearing,
weather, their old dreams.

27

LOGGING

1870. Ship spars for sailing ships.
The logs, close to the water.
The oxen yarded them.
The hand loggers with their axes, saws, Gilchrist jacks,
peevees. Five bucks a thousand feet.
The horse logging.
The logs peeled, put on skids, the skids greased.
Giants they were, piled to the sky.
Hand falling and bucking. With axes.
Springboards.
The loggers lined up at the cut, hats jaunty.
Smiling. By the cedar, 9 feet at the butt.
The sun shining through the old forest.
The lost forest.
The steam donkeys,
then the oil burners.
The diesels. The first bulldozers.
Then.
The sailing ships. Gone. The old forests.

LOGGING CAMPS

Meals announced by a gong
made from a sawblade.
Riggerman, fallers, buckers.
Ate like kings they did:
corned beef, ham, bacon, steak, chicken,
oysters, potatoes, boiled oats, sauerkraut,
carrots, turnips, breads, pies, doughnuts.
Bunk houses on skids,
some with 16 men.
Kerosene lamps,
a pot-bellied stove.
Lice. Bedbugs.
Many died.
The Chinese worked the greenchain,
the millpond. Their own bunkhouses.
Their language. Their ways.
Many died.

ED GILL AND THE ROAD BUILDING CREW 1900

He made the rounds   on a ladies bike,
wore a hat, a jacket, a fine beard. His crew wore hats,
vests, suspenders. The gentlemen
of the road, they were, with their wagons,
their horses. Built the roads around the giant trees,
the boulders they couldn't move.
35 cents an hour, 10 hour days.
For the feed bill. Just for the feed.

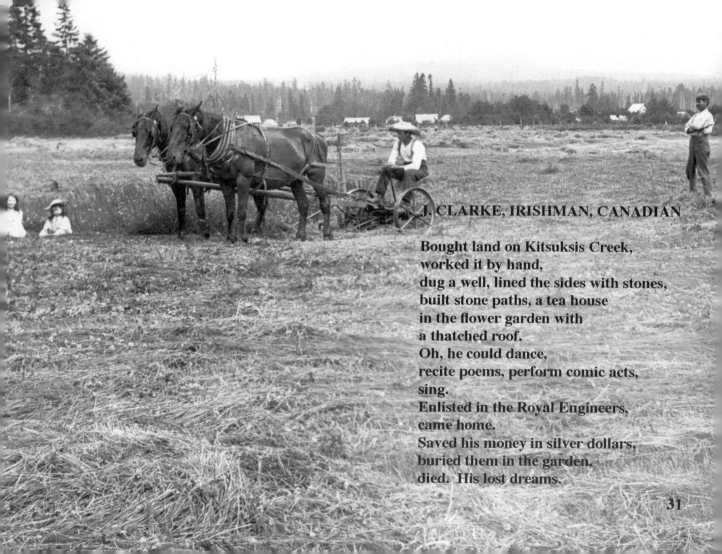

J. CLARKE, IRISHMAN, CANADIAN

Bought land on Kitsuksis Creek,
worked it by hand,
dug a well, lined the sides with stones,
built stone paths, a tea house
in the flower garden with
a thatched roof.
Oh, he could dance,
recite poems, perform comic acts,
sing.
Enlisted in the Royal Engineers,
came home.
Saved his money in silver dollars,
buried them in the garden,
died. His lost dreams.

31

THE HOLE ON JOHNSTON ROAD

The stagecoaches, the horses, the ox carts,
then the cars went around it.
It was fenced, still the children fell in,
the town drunks, a few cows, and 27 chickens, 12 ducks.
40 men and 11 teams of horses and wagons filled
the hole. And the ladies of the Community Club
came too with rum cake and carrot cake and hot tea.
Songs.
For the photograph the women wear white aprons.
Smile. The men behind them
wear hats and ties. Proud they were.

The Clarkes.
The Colemans.
The Cowleys.
The Drinkwaters.
The Goodalls.
The Grieves.
The Heaslips.
The Hills.
The Johnstons.
The McKenzies.
The Miles.
The Milligans.
The Pattersons.
The Phillips.
The Pineos.
The Richardsons.
The Sederholmes.
The Spencers.
The Taylors.
The Thompsons.
The Wests.
The Woodwards.
In their Sunday best.

ALBERNI, THE CITY

Wide streets where the cows pastured.
A firehall. Brigade. Red fire pails.
A water system from Roger Creek Falls.
Acre blocks. Waiting to be logged off.
The Arlington Hotel.
A new steam laundry.
For sale.

33

DREAMS CHANGE

The homemade oxcart. Gone.
The last horsedrawn stage to Nanaimo. Gone.
The E & N.
The first tractor (a Fordson with cleat wheels).
The men worked out on Government roads.
Lived on wild game: deer, salmon, grouse, duck, goose.
Their gardens.
The change.
The telephone.
The trucks.
The wide streets.
Stores.
New dreamers.

THE STATION

She has left the cacophony of bowls,
and is standing outside the station,
wearing a small knit hat,
tri-coloured, with an orange rose.
She wears a long white dress.
Small brown shoes.

Beside her is a man
wearing a buttoned vest.
His best tie. A cloth cap.
She holds his arm.
They are, between them,
a landscape.
They are the mud streets,
the half built houses.
They are their own history.
They are waiting for a train.

BEAVER CREEK

The oxen could make a return trip
in one day. They built a hall,
a school, store, post office. Meetings.
Someone brought out a harmonica,
someone played the ukulele.
Everyone sang.
When the cars arrived, they made the fast trip to town.
The store closed, the hall, the post office.
Dust.

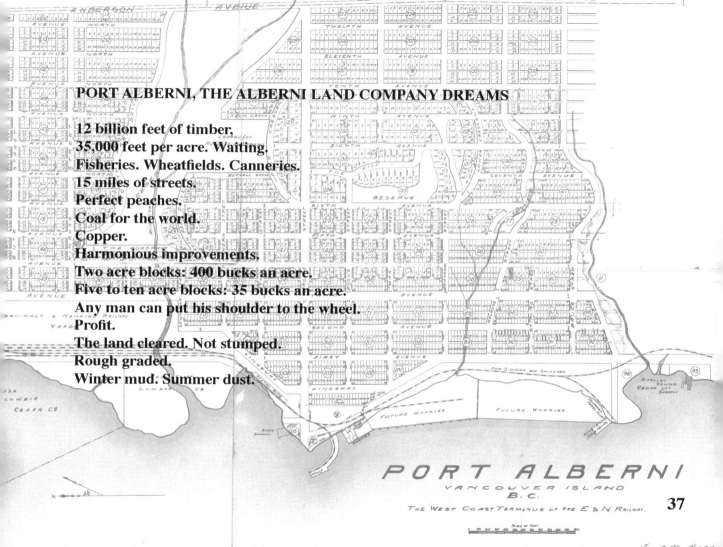

PORT ALBERNI, THE ALBERNI LAND COMPANY DREAMS

12 billion feet of timber,
35,000 feet per acre. Waiting.
Fisheries. Wheatfields. Canneries.
15 miles of streets.
Perfect peaches.
Coal for the world.
Copper.
Harmonious improvements.
Two acre blocks: 400 bucks an acre.
Five to ten acre blocks: 35 bucks an acre.
Any man can put his shoulder to the wheel.
Profit.
The land cleared. Not stumped.
Rough graded.
Winter mud. Summer dust.

ALBERNI PACIFIC LUMBER CO. CAMP 1, BEAVER CREEK, ALBERNI, 1940

There were 11 locomotives on
25 miles of track from bush to log dump.
The cookhouse crew, 14 Chinese,
served the finest food anywhere.
In the bunkhouse there was
Old Charlie, an ex-teamster and
three-fingered Joe,
who could still rig a spar tree,
and Hank, the chief bootlegger with his
home brew.
One retired minister for odd-jobs.
One noted foot racer.
One acclaimed swimmer from Ontario.
And Dunc, who could swear
in French and English, and never bathed,
from one year to the next.
All the exquisite bull peddlers
until lights out.

There were train wrecks,
and walking 10 miles to camp in the cold rain.
Sometimes logs rolled over the men,
riggers fell out of spar trees,
branches fell in the high winds, the widow makers.
Everyone listened for the misery whistle.
Some died.

THE PLYWOOD GIRLS

were not the ones appointed
to decorate the church,
to make wreaths at Christmas,
to spend their evenings
on a delightful midnight sleigh ride,
or go out with the bank manager's
wife to pick maidenhair ferns.
No.
They were the plywood girls,
hired in 1942 by Alberni Plywood.
If you were 16 and
could lift veneer,
layer it into sheets,
bundle plywood,
load boxcars
for 37 cents an hour,
the job was yours.
280 were hired.

By 1971, there were 30 women left.
Most on graveyard.
The Plywood bags,
they called them.
Stay home, their mothers said.
Stay home. Bake cakes. Be quiet.
Clean the house.
Watch out for your dreams.

39

MCLEAN MILL

The sawmill, a small village, wood cabins
by the stream, the steam donkey, the steam.
Loading their own train with lumber to Bainbridge,
to ship it out.
They logged by "the Gutless Wonder",
pulling the giant fir through the bare valleys.
Their cabins, the evening cedar.
The quiet of their dreams. The moon.

ANOTHER LANGUAGE

In the woods they used to say:
Bundle Stiff
Dragsaw
Gandy Dancer
Gut Hammer
Mulligan Car
Whistle Punk
Snoose, Skookum, Windjammer.
Now they say these corporate words:
Integrated
Dimensional lumber
Value added
Financial Ratio Analysis
Crown Harvest Rights
Remanufacturing
Windfall.

SAY THESE WORDS

The white man will teach your children to
read printing, and to be like themselves.
— *Gilbert Sproat, 1868*

Say Tseshaht, Hupacasath, Ahousaht,
Nuu-Chah-Nulth.
Say canoe, salmon,
baskets made of spruce root, cedar.
Say Potlatch, feast.
Say Reservation. Say tuberculosis.
Smallpox. Alcohol.

Say the children.
Raised with the sacred,
the ravens, the seasons of the moon,
to honour the earth, the elders.
Say Residential School.
The men who came in gunboats,
to take the children.
Say hunger. Say death.
Say the dark things without names.
Say these words.

42

The Stories

VIOLET

My mother worked the canneries,
we moved up and down the coast.
I was seven when the Indian Agent came.
The Port Alberni Residential School.
All those words. So lonely. My sister,
in another dorm.
One of the men hit me with a cane.
Once I got slapped.
The boys had it worse.
We all had our chores. Worked so hard.
I couldn't speak my language.
Later, we had to take the bus to school.
We spoke in whispers. We found ways.
My children lost their language.
My children.

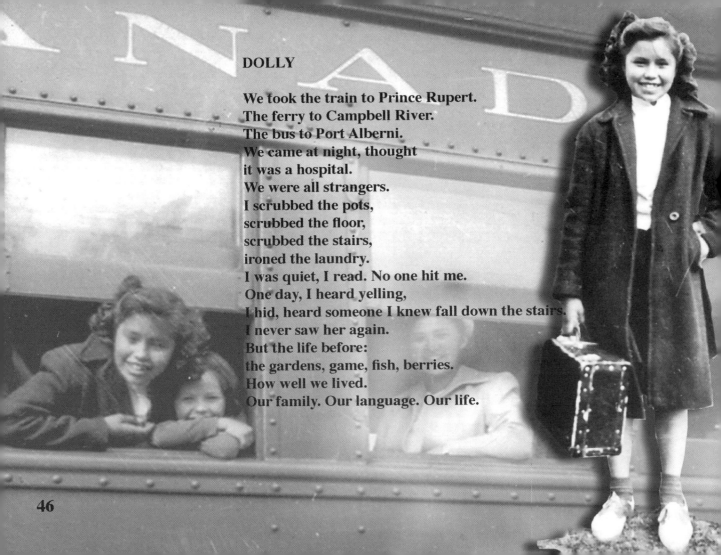

DOLLY

We took the train to Prince Rupert.
The ferry to Campbell River.
The bus to Port Alberni.
We came at night, thought
it was a hospital.
We were all strangers.
I scrubbed the pots,
scrubbed the floor,
scrubbed the stairs,
ironed the laundry.
I was quiet, I read. No one hit me.
One day, I heard yelling,
I hid, heard someone I knew fall down the stairs.
I never saw her again.
But the life before:
the gardens, game, fish, berries.
How well we lived.
Our family. Our language. Our life.

JOSEPHINE

My grandmothers wove baskets
decorated with killer whales, canoes.
I watched them, learned.
When I was 8 my father took me to
the school. If I spoke one word of Indian
I got strapped. When I got out,
I still had some words.
Went to work in the cannery.
Married Daniel. He was a fisherman.
He got drunk. Drowned.
I came to Port Alberni,
I was a waitress, a chambermaid.
I like to work.
Then I married Archie, he was a fisherman.
He died, not so long ago.
I still speak my Indian pretty good.
I love to read.
I used to weave baskets too. But my hands.
Now, I can't do it. My mind remembers.

HUGHIE

I saw my grandma die.
She had her raincoat over her head,
was going to take me across the Somass
in her canoe. A car hit her.
We had our language.
Our life.
In September, 1940, the Indian Agent
went from house to house.
Grabbed the kids. Residential School.
I cried every night.
I got TB in 1942, went to the hospital by steamship, train.
All the aboriginal kids there. I cried again. Stayed in bed
all the time. Some kids died.
I got better, went back to the school. One supervisor,
he was nice to me, gave me newspapers. Then he touched me.
Later, I tried to sneak out. I got whipped. We were hungry.
We took food out of garbage cans, stole beets, potatoes from
gardens. Roasted them over an open fire. We remembered.
Even in winter, we ate rotten apples. Got caught, strapped with
a horse harness. My hands bleeding.
They took my language. They took it.

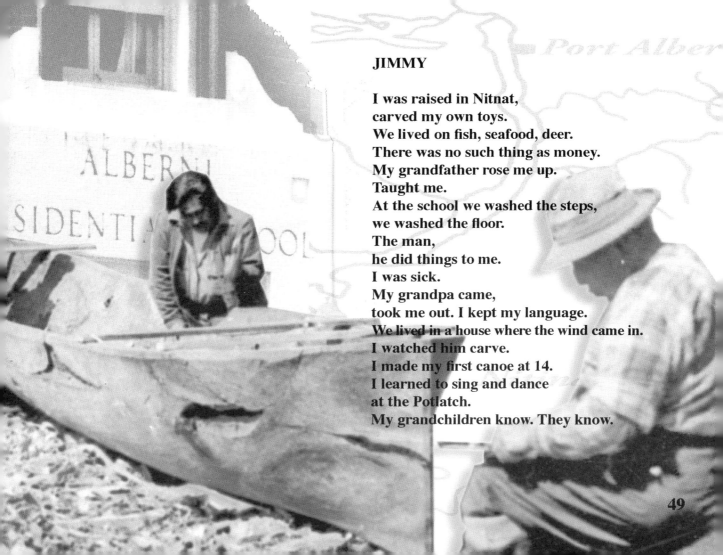

JIMMY

I was raised in Nitnat,
carved my own toys.
We lived on fish, seafood, deer.
There was no such thing as money.
My grandfather rose me up.
Taught me.
At the school we washed the steps,
we washed the floor.
The man,
he did things to me.
I was sick.
My grandpa came,
took me out. I kept my language.
We lived in a house where the wind came in.
I watched him carve.
I made my first canoe at 14.
I learned to sing and dance
at the Potlatch.
My grandchildren know. They know.

49

GEORGE

When I was born
my mother went to Nettle Island,
showed me to our people. She told me this.
I grew up on River Road.
I don't want to remember those years
at Residential School.
At home, we didn't speak our language.
My parents knew we'd be beaten for it.
My dad hitchhiked to Victoria.
Got us out, into public school. He was a fisherman,
a pile driver. Broke his back. He was always an artist.
He got famous.
I quit school in '55. Worked
in the plywood mill, at the fish packers,
the sawmill. We always sat at the back
of the bus. What do people see when they see us?
A drunk Indian? Nobody says it. It's hidden.
If you listen, you can hear it.

LARRY

My Uncle Bert, the head chief
of the Toquaht Nation, he asked
if I would learn
the Thunderbird dance. Headdress. Singing.
I practiced. Over and over.
Under the moon I danced. Under nights of stars.
By the shore I danced. In the fields.
Then I danced for my uncle in Nitnat.
He gave me one of his names, "Aniitsachist".
"I alone own the sea".

HELEN

We wore aprons. Cooked. Cleaned.
In 1952 it was a boomtown.
Schools were full.
Business was good.
Wives stayed home.
We entertained. Mixed the drinks.
We didn't borrow from the bank.
We saved up for the washing machine.
We knew about curtains and draperies.
We could iron.
We scrubbed the windows of our hearts.
Everybody had a car, a house, a boat.
Life was safe.
We didn't know we were building a dream.
We went to dances at the Greenwood Hotel.
The Rosebank.
The Policeman's Ball.
We got dressed up. Had our hair done.
We didn't know.

PAT

I bought a 1953 green Pontiac from my friend Yokum.
He'd run it into a pole, smashed up the front end pretty good.
So I got another Pontiac, replaced it. Took the nuns
from the Catholic school for rides, black flying
out of the windows like prayer flags.
One day I came in late, said I'd been at the A&W.
I'd been at the Barclay for a couple of beers.
I didn't last long there.
Went to work in the woods.
Whistleman, chokerman, rigger-slinger.
80 bucks a week.
On weekends we drank beer, chased girls,
shot grouse. Then.
The pulp mill.
Anybody could get a job.
Start on Tuesday, they said.
We did.

MARLENE

My dad was a carpenter.
He was one quarter Metis.
Played the guitar, the fiddle.
Had a radio show on CJAV, every Saturday
at 7 pm. I sang.
My husband's grandfather built our house
in 1912. I raised four kids, four foster kids,
had a big garden, chickens,
never enough time.
I'd make 30 loaves of bread a week,
wax the floors on my hands and knees.
When he said, "no wife of mine is going to work",
I left.

FRED

I used to roam around with Greta and Mary.
On Sundays, we'd go up China Creek,
inside the old mine tunnels.
There's gold in those rocks.
Gold. We knew it. Greta had a rock saw.
We used it. If we didn't find anything,
well, we'd have a picnic lunch.
Make a fire, toast cheese sandwiches
on a forked stick. Make tea.
Some days we panned for gold.
Found some.
I've got 5 tons of rock
just around my house.
You never know.

EILEEN

I've just lived my life.
I was a psychiatric nurse first.
Then I married a logger, he worked
in Franklin River, came home every six days.
That lasted three long years. The drinking, the shouting.
I joined a girl's band, played the drums.
Worked for the IWA, all that labour strife.
I was a night nurse for the plywood girls.
Had my own house, paid 25 bucks a month.
Then the three years on the tuna boat,
with the ex-funeral director. Got pregnant, left.
Then he sent me a telegram, "Let's tie the knot."
We did.
Later, we went to Bella Coola. He wanted to build
a furniture store. I didn't. We split.
The last one, well, I guess I'd always fancied him.
Used to be a trainman, I'd wave at him when he
was on the engine. He was a real
union guy, a good Commie, they said.
I've just lived my life.

DAN

In 1950, I was 15, pushed lumber on rollers,
picked up railway ties off the greenchain.
McLean Mill. My dad came to work there
in 1926. Wanted a union. They fired him,
black listed him. He rode his bike to Great Central Lake
for a job he didn't get. Had to go on relief.
2 years. 15 bucks a month.
Those days.

DON

My great grandfather's uncle,
pre-empted 300 acres. 1870.
Cleared the land. Started a house.
Got sick. Sent a letter to Australia.
My great grandfather arrived in 1882.
Finished the house. Sent for his wife and kids.
They came by boat to San Francisco, then to Victoria,
that took 3 months, then by coal barge to Qualicum.
They walked to Horne Lake. He found them.
They died young.
When I was 12 in 1944, I worked at
McLean Mill. Got the hard jobs,
everything pushed by hand,
loaded railway cars with ties, lumber.
I tailed the edger, worked the boom.
We were the horses there,
some died, worked themselves to death.
My grandfather, he helped build the roads,
with horse and wagon. I knew hard work. I knew.

JOHN

I have so many dreams.
But I'm no artist.
I'm no poet. But I want a world that's
green, and nobody's poor. I'm the dreamer.
I want to see a bridge
over Roger's Creek. People on bikes,
people walking across the bridge
from one side of Port to the other.
Once we were one of the richest towns
in Canada. The mills. Everybody had a car.
A valley full of hope. Money. Their own dreams.
Now.
I dream festivals, bridges. For this valley.
I dream.

Photo Credits

49	Pat	Smith Memorial School Nuns AVM PN11680
		Redford Street at Third Avenue AVM PN9339
50	Marlene	Photographs from private collection
51	Fred	China Creek Mining Map 1895 AVM
		Mine entrance at China Creek AVM PN7564
		Gold panning women AVM PN13824
52	Eileen	Photographs from private collection
53	Dan	Great Central Lake townsite AVM PN5925
		Loading lumber at McLean Mill AVM PN5057
54	Don	McLean Mill AVM PN5073
		Lumber on deck AVM PN11886
55	John	New bridge on Third Avenue AVM PN3780

(AVM = Alberni Valley Museum)

After

word

I'm always delighted by the surprises that arrive in my path. Take, for instance one spring evening I was roaming around Value Village in Kamloops. A fellow went by with a cart full of books, and on top was a beat up big book with red covers with printing on it. As he went by, I grabbed it. It was the 1922 Wrigley's B.C. Directory. Not only did it list every town in B.C., but it had the names and occupations of the residents. I opened it and it fell open to the Alberni section: "When the visitor arrives in the Alberni Valley he realizes what the feelings of the poet, Tom Moore, were when he viewed the Vale of Avoca, 'There is not in the wide world a valley so sweet.'" This was a treasure. I had to have it. After some negotiating with the book cart guy who said the book person wouldn't be in until the next day to price it, I just gave him 10 bucks and took it with me.

In July of 2007, since I was to be a host for the opening night of Forest Fest in Port Alberni, I thought I ought to write a poem using the information in the Alberni and Port Alberni sections from the Directory. And so I wrote, in part:

I would have liked to be there, in 1922
where I could have found two first class
*   tourist hotels,*
(the Somass Hotel at 4 bucks a day)
a moving picture theatre,
adequate retail stores for 1000 people.
Would I have known Myrtle Anderson,
waitress at the King Edward Hotel,
Minnie Munday, B.C. Telephone agent,

Eliza Bryant, who ran a rooming house,
or James Duncan, harness and shoe
*   maker,*
Doris Higginbottom of Hub Bakery,
or Tom Wong of the Teakettle Inn Café?

Jean McIntosh, director of the Alberni Valley Museum, heard me read the poem and the next day, while I was sitting in one of the logger's shacks at McLean Mill writing poems for anyone who came by, she came in. She said, "let's do something for the Museum, maybe write poems of the history of the valley." I said yes, right away, not knowing then what that yes would mean.

What it meant was that I, in a sense, would go to the Alberni Valley in 1858 to the present. I sailed into the lives of the residents there through journals and archival photos. I imagined their lives as I wrote the poems. I talked to First Nations residents and began to understand how the lives of their ancestors had been changed forever by the arrival of the European settlers.

In 1876, the government of Canada introduced the Indian Act, which became law. It provided Canada's federal government exclusive authority to legislate in relation to "Indians and lands reserved for Indians".

It was amended in 1927 "any parent or guardian refusing to send their children to Residential School will face a fine or imprisonment for a term not exceeding 10 days or both and such child may be arrested without warrant and conveyed to the school by a truant officer."

I understood the destructive consequences of Residential Schools on those I spoke to.

When the exhibit opened on March 28, 2008, I was amazed to see my poems on the walls, on photographs, next to photographs. Cindy Van Volsem, the curator at the Museum had matched my poems to photos. They, in a sense, became a third thing, a photo/poem.

I wanted a book of photo/poems. And I wanted to write poems for the current residents of the Valley, who had memories of their lives there, or the lives of their fathers. I talked to survivors of Residential School, to those who had worked at McLean Mill, to housewives, to miners. What they told me changed me: changed my view of Canada, changed my understanding of the lives of

First Nations people, whose history on the West Coast of Vancouver Island goes back over 4,000 years. They came to the Museum with their photos, we sat in two big chairs and they told me their stories. In a sense, these poems gave them a voice. And their voices were sometimes filled with the pain of their memories. Similarly, the poems I wrote for the exhibit gave voice to the ghosts of those who first came to the valley. What were their dreams?

I would like to thank my publisher, Marty Gervais, who has been publishing beautiful books for 40 years, for thinking this book might give its readers a view of a world that is, in a real sense, the history of Canada. I would also like to thank Jean McIntosh, for creating a beautiful exhibit and having a delicious vision of this project and Jamie Morton (who is not related to me) for his historic overview. And thanks to Shelly Harding and Kirsten Smith for their hard work in creating the exhibit. Cindy Van Volsem deserves great thanks for taking my poems, searching through the archival photographs to find the perfect photographs to match the poems. And for taking the photographs I was given by those I interviewed and seamlessly placing the poems on them.

I would have known them all,
in this place of valleys and mountains,
this place at the water's edge.

Wendy Morton
April, 2009